DISCOVERING THE UNITED STATES

Kentucky

BY CANDICE RANSOM

Kids Core
An Imprint of Abdo Publishing
abdobooks.com

abdobooks.com

Published by Abdo Publishing, a division of ABDO, PO Box 398166, Minneapolis, Minnesota 55439. Copyright © 2025 by Abdo Consulting Group, Inc. International copyrights reserved in all countries. No part of this book may be reproduced in any form without written permission from the publisher. Kids Core™ is a trademark and logo of Abdo Publishing.

Printed in the United States of America, North Mankato, Minnesota.
052024
092024

THIS BOOK CONTAINS RECYCLED MATERIALS

Cover Photo: Steve Robinson/Shutterstock Images
Interior Photos: Pictures Now/Alamy, 4–5; Bonnie Taylor Barry/Shutterstock Images, 7 (top left); Jon Benedictus/Shutterstock Images, 7 (top right); Alexei Korshunov/Shutterstock Images, 7 (bottom left); Azahara Perez/Shutterstock Images, 7 (bottom right); Alexey Stiop/Shutterstock Images, 9, 26; Sean Pavone/iStockphoto, 10, 29 (bottom left); Shutterstock Images, 12–13; iStockphoto, 15, 18; Stanley Weston Archive/Archive Photos/Getty Images, 16; Leonid Andronov/Shutterstock Images, 20–21; Ko Zatu/Shutterstock Images, 22; Nagel Photography/Shutterstock Images, 25; Red Line Editorial, 28 (left), 29 (top); Sean Pavone/Shutterstock Images, 28 (right); Anthony Delgado/Shutterstock Images, 29 (bottom right)

Editor: Laura Stickney
Series Designer: Katharine Hale

Library of Congress Control Number: 2023949356

Publisher's Cataloging-in-Publication Data

Names: Ransom, Candice, author.
Title: Kentucky / by Candice Ransom.
Description: Minneapolis, Minnesota: Abdo Publishing, 2025 | Series: Discovering the United States | Includes online resources and index.
Identifiers: ISBN 9781098293871 (lib. bdg.) | ISBN 9798384913146 (ebook)
Subjects: LCSH: U.S. states--Juvenile literature. | Kentucky--History--Juvenile literature. | Southeastern States--Juvenile literature. | Physical geography--United States--Juvenile literature.
Classification: DDC 973--dc23

All population data taken from:
"Estimates of Population by Sex, Race, and Hispanic Origin: April 1, 2020 to July 1, 2022." *US Census Bureau, Population Division*, June 2023, census.gov.

CONTENTS

CHAPTER 1
The Kentucky Derby 4

CHAPTER 2
The People of Kentucky 12

CHAPTER 3
Places in Kentucky 20

State Map 28
Glossary 30
Online Resources 31
Learn More 31
Index 32
About the Author 32

Oliver Lewis sits atop Aristides after the pair won the first Kentucky Derby in 1875.

The Kentucky Derby

It was May 17, 1875. Fifteen Thoroughbred horses and their riders waited on a dirt track. They were about to compete in the first Kentucky Derby. At the starter's signal, the horses and **jockeys** sped down the track. A crowd of 10,000 people cheered them on.

The horses raced 1.5 miles (2.4 km). After about two and a half minutes, a horse named Aristides won. His jockey was 19-year-old Oliver Lewis.

Today, the Kentucky Derby is the most famous horse race in the United States. It takes place at Churchill Downs in Louisville, Kentucky. The race is held on the first Saturday in May. Many fans

The Triple Crown

The Triple Crown is a horse racing championship for Thoroughbred horses. It includes three races: the Kentucky Derby, the Preakness Stakes, and the Belmont Stakes. If a horse wins all three races in a year, it wins the Triple Crown. In 1919, the horse Sir Barton became the first Triple Crown winner. Justify became the thirteenth Triple Crown winner in 2018.

Kentucky Facts

DATE OF STATEHOOD
June 1, 1792

CAPITAL
Frankfort

POPULATION
4,512,310

AREA
40,408 square miles
(104,656 sq km)

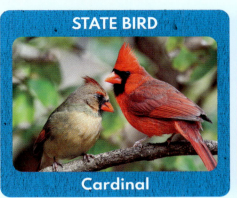
STATE BIRD
Cardinal

STATE TREE
Tulip poplar

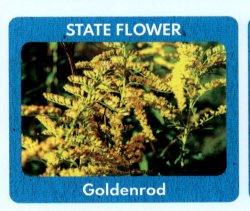
STATE FLOWER
Goldenrod

STATE HORSE
Thoroughbred

Each US state has a different population, size, and capital city. States also have state symbols.

gather to watch it. Some wear colorful hats. The horses and jockeys line up at the starting gate. They race 1.25 miles (2 km). The winning horse and jockey are given a **garland** of red roses.

The Derby is often called the Greatest Two Minutes in Sports. It is a Kentucky tradition.

Kentucky's Land

Kentucky is in the US region called the South. Ohio and Indiana border the state to the north. Missouri and Illinois lie to the west. To the east are West Virginia and Virginia, and to the south is Tennessee. Eastern Kentucky is home to the Cumberland **Plateau**. This rocky region is part of the Appalachian Mountains.

Kentucky's land includes mountains, forests, rivers, and grasslands. It is nicknamed the Bluegrass State. This is because the state's meadows are covered with bluegrass. This deep green grass is used to **graze** cows

Kentucky bluegrass is the most common planting grass in the United States.

and horses. Other animals in the state include deer, gray squirrels, and cardinals. The Ohio River divides Kentucky and Ohio. The Mississippi flows along Kentucky's western border.

Cumberland Falls State Resort Park is known as the Niagara of the South.

Climate

Kentucky has four seasons and a humid climate. Rainfall is common throughout the year. In the spring, plants grow. Summers in Kentucky are long and hot.

In the fall, trees have brightly colored leaves. Winters are mild. Heavy snow comes to the northern and eastern mountains.

Explore Online

Visit the website below. Does it give more information about the Kentucky Derby that wasn't in Chapter One?

Kentucky Derby

abdocorelibrary.com/discovering-kentucky

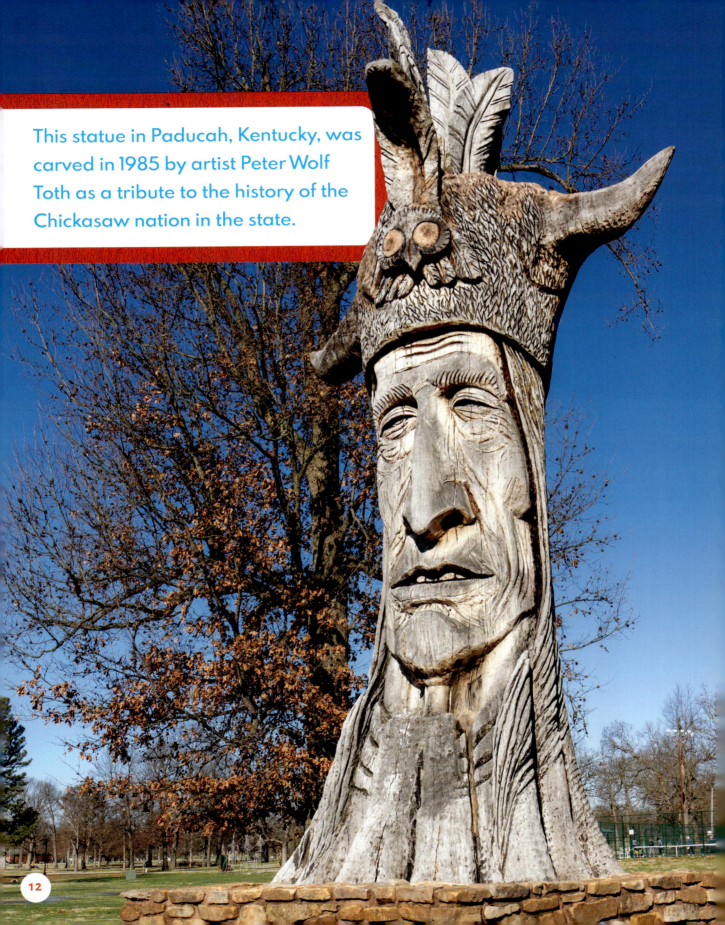

This statue in Paducah, Kentucky, was carved in 1985 by artist Peter Wolf Toth as a tribute to the history of the Chickasaw nation in the state.

CHAPTER 2

The People of Kentucky

American Indians have lived in Kentucky for more than 12,000 years. By the 1500s, the largest groups in the state were the Cherokee, Chickasaw, and Shawnee nations. They hunted, fished, and grew crops.

In the late 1600s and 1700s, white **settlers** came to Kentucky. Many were **fur trappers**. They came from eastern states such as Pennsylvania and North Carolina.

In the late 1700s, people passed into Kentucky through the Cumberland Gap. This passage cuts through the Appalachian Mountains. Many settlers brought enslaved Black people to Kentucky to work on farms.

Wilderness Road

In the 1700s, the Appalachian Mountains were hard to cross. In 1775, explorer Daniel Boone and other men built a road through the Cumberland Gap. They called it the Wilderness Road.

The Kentucky state flag depicts an image of a frontiersman, *left*, shaking hands with a politician.

As more settlers arrived, they forced American Indians to move off their homelands.

Today, Kentucky's population is 83 percent white. Nine percent of Kentuckians are Black, and 2 percent are Asian. About 4 percent are Hispanic or Latino. Less than 1 percent are American Indian.

Muhammad Ali won the heavyweight championship of the world three times in the 1960s and 1970s.

Famous Kentuckians include Abraham Lincoln, the sixteenth US president. Lincoln was born in Hardin County, Kentucky, in 1809. The famous boxer Muhammad Ali was born in Louisville in 1942.

Culture

Kentucky is famous for its music. Early settlers and enslaved people sang **ballads**. In 1938,

Bill Monroe formed the Blue Grass Boys band. He sang high-pitched songs that told stories. This music style became known as bluegrass.

Kentucky's culture can also be seen in its food. One common dish is chocolate walnut derby pie. Another is spoon bread. It is a soft, fluffy bread made with cornmeal.

College basketball is very popular in Kentucky. The University of Kentucky has won eight men's basketball titles. The University of Louisville has won two championships.

Industry

Many Kentuckians work in **manufacturing**, creating products such as cars. General Motors makes Corvettes in the city of Bowling Green.

There are more than 35,000 horse farms in Kentucky.

Georgetown, Kentucky, is home to the world's largest Toyota car factory.

Other industries include coal mining and farming. Farms produce corn, soybeans, and tobacco. Kentuckians also raise horses and cattle. Many people work on the army bases of Fort Knox and Fort Campbell.

Primary Source

Kentuckian Doug Naselroad founded a school that teaches people how to make instruments, such as guitars. He said:

> I love the creative dynamic of [making musical instruments]. You start with a chunk of wood and you end up with a song. I mean that's magic, it really is!

Source: "Humans of Central Appalachia—Our Stories: Doug Naselroad." *Humans of Central Appalachia,* 22 Jan. 2016, humansofcentralappalachia.org. Accessed 18 Sept. 2023.

Point of View

What is the author's point of view on this topic? What is your point of view? Write a short essay about how they are similar and different.

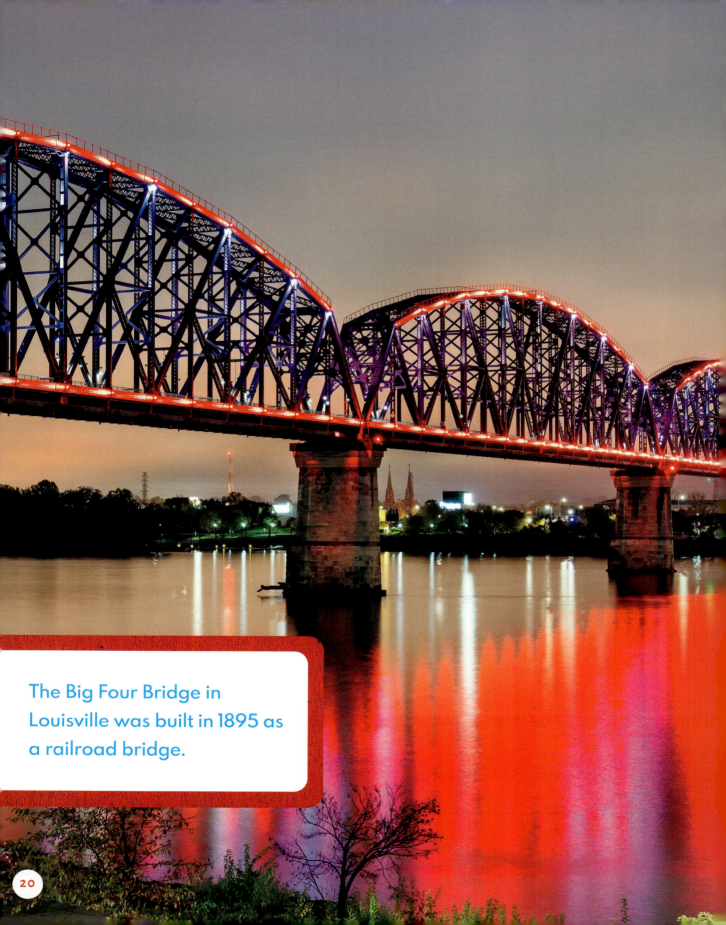

The Big Four Bridge in Louisville was built in 1895 as a railroad bridge.

CHAPTER 3

Places in Kentucky

Kentucky's capital is Frankfort. It is located in the northern part of the state on the Kentucky River. Louisville is the state's largest city. The Big Four Bridge crosses the Ohio River. It connects Louisville to Jeffersonville, Indiana. People can walk or bike across it.

Mammoth Cave National Park was named a World Heritage site in 1981.

The city of Lexington is home to the Kentucky Horse Park. People can visit museums and learn about 50 different horse breeds. The Keeneland racecourse is also in Lexington. Horse races are held there.

Parks

Kentucky has several national parks and state parks. One is Mammoth Cave National Park. Mammoth Cave is the longest known cave system on Earth. It formed millions of years ago when rainwater flowed through rock beds. This created tunnels and other formations.

Cave Guides

In the 1800s and 1900s, Mammoth Cave was on private land. White owners made enslaved Black people work as tour guides in the cave. Mat Bransford was one of those guides. His son and his grandson also became tour guides. Today, guide Jerry Bransford tells visitors about his family's story.

People have mapped more than 400 miles (644 km) of the cave. Visitors can take tours of it.

At Cumberland Falls State Resort Park, people can see Kentucky's biggest waterfall. It is one of the only places in the world where visitors can see moonbows. These kinds of rainbows form on nights with a full moon. Moonbows are caused when moonlight is bent through water droplets.

The Abraham Lincoln Birthplace National Historical Park honors the sixteenth US president. He was president from 1861 to 1865. The park includes a memorial with 56 steps, which represent Lincoln's 56 years of life. Inside, people can see a cabin that looks like the one in which Lincoln was born.

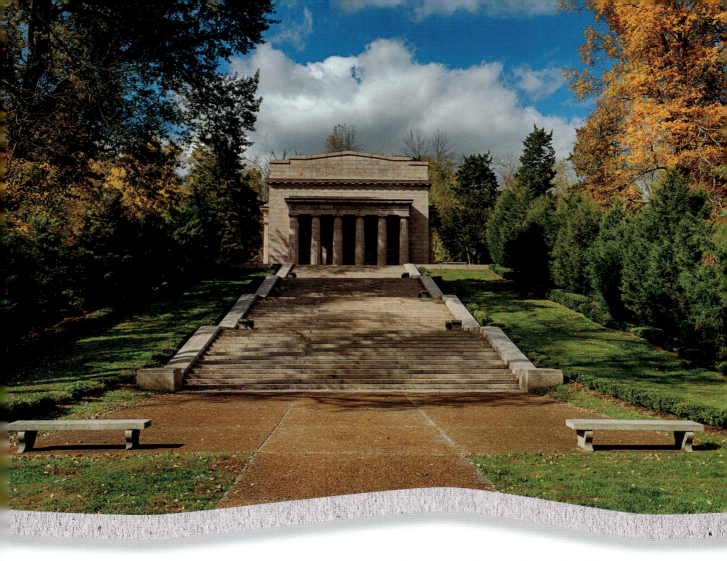

Abraham Lincoln lived in Kentucky from birth until just before his eighth birthday, when his family moved to Indiana.

Landmarks

In Louisville, people can visit the Louisville Slugger Museum and Factory. They can learn about how wooden baseball bats are made.

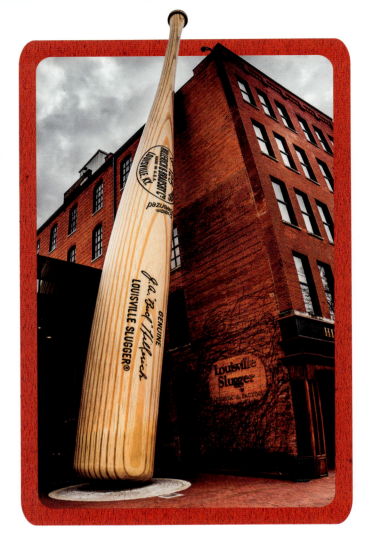

The Hillerich & Bradsby Company has been making Louisville Slugger bats for professional baseball players since 1884.

The museum is also home to the world's biggest baseball bat. It stands 120 feet (37 m) tall and weighs 68,000 pounds (30,800 kg).

Another Kentucky landmark is Fort Knox. It is the most secure military base in the United States. Its vault holds nearly $300 billion in gold bars. Visitors can't go inside Fort Knox, but they can take pictures at its gate.

Kentucky is full of exciting things to see and do. Visitors can explore the state's parks. They can learn about the state's history. No matter what people are interested in, all kinds of adventures await in Kentucky.

Further Evidence

Look at the website below, which contains a map of Kentucky's state parks. Does it give any new evidence to support Chapter Three?

Kentucky State Parks: Maps

abdocorelibrary.com/discovering-kentucky

State Map

KEY
 Capital Park
City or town Point of interest

Louisville

Kentucky: The Bluegrass State

Cumberland Falls State Resort Park

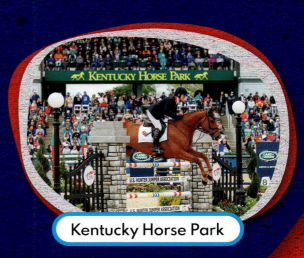
Kentucky Horse Park

Glossary

ballads
slow songs that tell a story

fur trappers
people who hunt and trap animals and trade their furs

garland
a wreath that combines flowers with leaves, which people wear or hang as a decoration

graze
to let animals feed on something throughout the day

jockey
a person who rides a horse in a race

manufacturing
the process of making goods to sell

plateau
an area of land that is high and flat

settlers
people who moved to a new area

Online Resources

To learn more about Kentucky, visit our free resource websites below.

Visit **abdocorelibrary.com** or scan this QR code for free Common Core resources for teachers and students, including vetted activities, multimedia, and booklinks, for deeper subject comprehension.

Visit **abdobooklinks.com** or scan this QR code for free additional online weblinks for further learning. These links are routinely monitored and updated to provide the most current information available.

Learn More

Mazzarella, Kerri. *Thoroughbred.* Crabtree, 2024.

Murray, Julie. *Kentucky.* Abdo, 2020.

Payne, Stefanie. *The National Parks.* DK, 2020.

Index

Cherokee people, 13
Chickasaw people, 13
Cumberland Plateau, 8

food, 17–18
forts, 18, 26–27
Frankfort, 7, 21

industry, 17–18

Kentucky Derby, 5–8

Lexington, 22
Lincoln, Abraham, 16, 24
Louisville, 6, 16–17, 21, 25

music, 16–17, 19

parks, 23–24, 27

rivers, 9, 21

Shawnee people, 13
sports, 5–8, 16–17, 25–26
state symbols, 7

Triple Crown, 6

About the Author

Candice Ransom is an author. She has visited Kentucky several times.